Where I Came Here From

poems by

Christopher Burawa

Finishing Line Press
Georgetown, Kentucky

Where I Came Here From

Copyright © 2023 by Christopher Burawa
ISBN 979-8-88838-184-7 First Edition
All rights reserved under International and Pan-American Copyright Conventions. No part of this book may be reproduced in any manner whatsoever without written permission from the publisher, except in the case of brief quotations embodied in critical articles and reviews.

ACKNOWLEDGMENTS

General acknowledgement is made to the editors of the following publications, in which some of these poems first appeared.

Blackbird: Condolence for the Blind Mori
Burnside Review: An Enso for Larry Levis
Columbia Poetry Review: The Mind Flows a River that Murders Someone
Del Sol Review: Silent Zoo; Taxidermist's Cat
Hayden's Ferry Review: Dripping Surgery
Moments of the Soul: Poems of Meditation and Mindfulness. An Unfolding from Zero (published as, For Ghosts Clinging to Trees and Grasses)
Prairie Schooner: A Theory of Eczema; Neighbors Rising above Octaves
Superstition Review: Actually, This Is West of My Dwelling Place (published as, Act of Ghosting to Avoid Complications); Like a Good Horse; Vultures and the Constant Application of Them; Regret, Speckled by Want
Whisky Island Review: Doubts and the Need to Know (published as, To naked men, to women naked as rain)

I want to express my deep thanks to my friends Cynthia Hogue and Melissa Cundieff who helped me in innumerable ways in preparing this manuscript. My thanks to master printmaker and friend, Steven Sorman, for allowing me use of his artwork, "Sandstone" for the cover image.

Publisher: Leah Huete de Maines
Editor: Christen Kincaid
Cover Art: Steven Sorman, "Sandstone"
Author Photo: Eydís Burawa
Cover Design: Elizabeth Maines McCleavy

Order online: www.finishinglinepress.com
also available on amazon.com

Author inquiries and mail orders:
Finishing Line Press
PO Box 1626
Georgetown, Kentucky 40324
USA

Table of Contents

An Unfolding from Zero xi

The Mind Flows a River that Murders Someone 1

Neighbors Rising above Octaves 2

Where I Came Here From 3

Actually, This Is West of My Dwelling Place 6

Condolence for the Blind Mori 7

An Enso for Larry Levis 8

Doubts and the Need to Know 10

The Solitary 11

Antidote to the Chaos of Imagination 12

Dripping Surgery 13

Silent Zoo 14

An Icelandic Christmas Poem without Animals 15

The Taxidermist's Cat 16

A Theory of Eczema 17

Bobby Fischer Dies during the Whaling Report 18

Like a Good Horse 20

Regret, Speckled by Want 21

Vultures and the Constant Application of Them 23

Agrimensura of the Mire: Árnessysla 24

Notes 26

*For my late teacher and Dharma friend
Norman Dubie*

An Unfolding from Zero

Thought is struggle. And what you call
life is thought. And the hum of needing

to interpret life ends when thinking ends,

and so thinking is interpreting the hum
that manifests the place where you are.

Fear creates the hum when,

after a time, you remember
to occupy the place you were last in

but forgot that you were somewhere

else. And if this sounds like a dream,
it's because your mind is as if in a dream.

You struggle to get back but really

don't have to because fear creates the
thought to go back and you do. Along

the way, it reassembles the past,

how you last remember what happened,
but is inexact. Then the cosmos breaks

open to let you through. Something is born.

Experience, sensation begins as if
reborn. The space around you is itself

reborn, and you inhabit it.

The Mind Flows a River that Murders Someone

I'll fold the door in half for you,
crease it with an elbow so as
to keep a face that greets
the world.

There had been all this talk about
the old miracle, when
you heal the lock,
you heal the forgiven.

But a river is a door
more than a window.

Close friends and relatives
might tell you otherwise, tell you
millions are falling in love with the idea,
that NASA
raved about the elastic physics,
the principles of temperature and
force behind the slightest
obligations.

Every water bird I've surveyed
ignored it. My drowned women ignore it.

Once, I stared at a river until I blacked out.
And it wasn't like a window slid open
to an abuzz. Sight

became sound into
a river.

Really, a river is a door,
until it opens.

Neighbors Rising above Octaves

The jarring detail suspected from the street

is how I hear you ridicule a vein,
beg it to be nice,
that most simplified of lies
governing all the shades of white
in a jeweler's handbag—which include
the orchestrated pinks and a token pearl.

We took a clumsy vote,
a raising of eyebrows,
and decided to audit your mad housework.

Stunned, you answered by shaving only with water.

How can we love you now, when all you do
is look east, toward
the worst star possible,
and pray that it will rise.

Where I Came Here From

1.
My father left me no stories
to tell you when
you ask me. And you
will ask. My past is part
of what I give you as I
steadily disappear. You will
want it and I will give you what
you ask.

I once saw a caterpillar eat
cat food, paring away into
its gut a sliver of chicken
like it would a leaf…

2.
My father's mantra was: *know
it for yourself.* But I have no
memory of him saying this to me,
in a room with a window facing a
bay where a pod of whales spend
the night, the setting sun rainbowing
red like a burst vein from their flukes.

He was kind mostly and urged me
to observation. When I was a boy,
scientists said we had yet to understand
outer space and the ocean depths, as if
we had pinned down all the rest.

3.
Now, I believe we don't even
know our own backyards. I am
learning about our new one in
Tennessee. The sluggish copperheads

I relocate to the ravine. The yellow chats
that steal the cat's dry food. The robins'
short détente in early spring.

When I tell you that shadows have
their own shadows you will know
this fact for yourself. That deer do not
eat every horse chestnut but
always plant one.

4.
Your grandfather has been dead
most of my life. I remember him
gentler now, which means
I grew to know him completely.
His father was a Prussian Army officer
and Cossack. His henchman emigrated
with him to New York City and bought
his drinks and spent years paying off
the debt. And the three of them
are with me now as I write this poem. We
found each other where all life goes, the
place where we all disappear.

5.
A small pollinating fly danced its courtship
on the deck chair just now. How beautiful. I hope
you see this dance yourself one day. The
scissoring wings alone. The female making
a circuit around him to know for herself…

Don't be frightened of my disappearing.
I have seen you do it myself many times
and know that as you grow you will forget
how to do it as easily as you do now. Just

know that you can, and that when you do
you will bring back some of its peace.
Then these words will mean nothing
and you will know for yourself how
the universe comes back with you.

Actually, This Is West of My Dwelling Place

The season contradicts the ration of mind.

Midnight's prologue mirroring the empty

tub and all its sad associations. An old-fashioned

mythology of, say, eyes. Eyes like ears. Or eyes

like a mouth, a boundary that casts off its reverse

without your effort. From the first, there is the rolling in

and rolling out. The frozen water and the waterfall

respond with sameness. Throughout the body

there are no reflected images. We meet spontaneously.

Ovations of wintering grapevines shouting

more heart…

Condolence for the Blind Mori

You will fall into a place
without bathrooms or salt.
It is the Mind without limits,
resting. What moments

before had been the active
bubble of the autumn tearoom
collapses into our shared home.
Your childhood drum is here,

the one-eyed cat is here,
your grandmother's favorite
stone is here. And Ikkyu waits,
but not as you remember him.

The embrace is the same,
so complete there is no need
to speak. But for you he did,
as you both separated, whispering

in your ear: *Whose eyes do not open?*

An Enso for Larry Levis

The moon died,
an odor of urine and bruised
parsley that attaches to the rims
of old jam jars. Everything

then becomes a setback,
complements often tucked together—

the white board

on which we used to write dispatches
is about to recall
a fallen center. Our lives,

before this moment, required a bit of acting—
the futured self standing alongside
the necessary past
like approving parents.

But behind them both
the night sky or a blue tacky
dawn embraces the perfect mallet

of scent, similar to the tincture

you prepared for weeds,
weeds that grow the length of all relations,

mimicking a doorway
where you watch the coming night,
equal inside and outside,

you unable to step through
what's not next:

the white bib of a certain
speckled bird that lives
only in your trees.

We're speaking of an event
that's an instruction,
if named, a faint corruption
of anticipation called "baby finds the tit."

And who doesn't wish?

Doubts and the Need to Know

It's not her fault she looks like Spencer Tracy
and he her because genius may be a matter

of luck. It's not her fault that he borrowed
the raincoat because the real thing can only

make it seem more as one who lives within
the character that understands beige

with wrinkles. The plop of a hat. A wink he stole.
The wink that won a woman who loved him

or her despite the thievery and borrowing because
what mattered was the love of the something

completely loving the coat as one making
and who thinks of how the excited pigeons flock

and flock around the feet expectant and hungry,
hungry enough to shit and thank god for the coat

because without it genius patrols the outskirts
of the park intent eventually pausing to believe

that the face she's expecting he owns.

The Solitary

Where there is only brutality, space directs response against political necessity, much as whole cream milk informs a dry brisket's gravy. Here who doesn't prefer following fragrant grasses and return pursuing the falling flowers? Why he studied old dogwoods prospering below curly maples. We could discuss the gradual going against the ordinary. But what then? Remove the right? Remove the left? Why a wilded garden acts as a better studio than a room but informs the room: a hanging lamp with the suspended bulb acting as the light of the past father and the fulsome rice-papered globe the future mother. We might as well be talking about birth or death, inviting disorder. Now he cuts off the tongues of everyone on earth.

Antidote to the Chaos of Imagination

Here, in Reykjavik,
rain has brought the seagulls down from foraging for
kittens. The great mountain Esja,

home to two giants—male and female—stopped being
a flat stone and has disappeared.

To the north, a sheep farmer in Arnarfjord

can't remember the last time he received
a visitor. He has no wife or heifer. On days like this,
he'll sit content at the kitchen window with his half
reflection, coffee, and a cigarette's ember all day.

Dripping Surgery

An impulse emerges within the Self as an appetite to be
the object it seeks, an oblique reference to, say, drift ice

and the silly muscle of weather that follows along. The white
relics on which we could step out on, an invented spirit realm,

thaw in mad abundance. With this act, a tenth of everything has
been sacrificed. So be it, because not far from Holar, holy see of

northern Iceland, in the land of the Skaga men, Catholic bishop
Guðbrandur has had a vision. A herd of fierce horses, eyes rolling

in the knuckles of their brows, run along the fields across
the river, toward the monastery. The river is in flood, but

they cross anyway, fetlocks working, they heave
above the water. Across, they run twice around the chapel,

clockwise. Guðbrandur runs and pulls himself onto the back
of the lead horse, a black with a white mane. All of this

is holy because he knows the horse by name, calls
it, bids the stallion to take him to every farm across Iceland.

Many people claim they saw him in their dreams, bestowing
blessings with a sword. *Paradise must be claimed*, his benediction.

The good bishop slaughters the horse to the bone, exhuming
the buttery reeds of marrow. He turns to his flock. *You will eat this.*

The Silent Zoo

Why stop at a stuffed donkey? A small room is only

limited by the lines and sawdust. Once the garage

is scuttled for a den, possibility crosses the room

like the taxidermist's wife. She's not exact, but clever.

So the lion overarching the desk is not so much leaping

as climbing the ladder. Genius like that is the poor vehicle

of the heart, presupposing another honest reaction.

Let's face it, we all love the wife. She would bleat

better than a goat standing in an ocean.

An Icelandic Christmas Poem without Animals

To talk about above and below is to miss the point,
gumming our own useless rye. Without the benefit
of a wife we might eat strange things,

things that make us remember what the mind
put a stop to, abject lessons that led us along
like a reinvented anthem or breathy hymn. And so,

the juleswain has been slain, sacrificed on the tiptoe,
given three days to rise and report gifts that might be
the dream of a daughter, when the other, the maid,

sometimes seen with a lantern, has other purposes
better than his. Her smile is better, rose lips offset
by starvation. He, on the other hand, has been overfed
since June, his offal, dried and braided, will burn
a propane red, the creeping flames marching.

We know his friendly names: Fence-Post,
Gully-Lad, Stump, Ladle-Licker, Sausage-
Grabber, Bowl-Licker, Window-Peeper, Candle-
Scrounger. Advancing his reputation.

But it's what we planned. There's no regimen
to a strategy of doubt—why the julemaid
holds up a light, to find the bluing skin of sleep…

And as you've suspected, there is a manger,
with a newborn pink and off-
steaming like a boiled beet.

His halo is a platter.
We're nourished by the infant mind.

The Taxidermist's Cat

A molar I dedicated to modern acts of camouflage,
and banned from my collection, has ceased.

Unsalvageable. With hairline fractures disappearing
into the fundament. It's neighbor, a baby tooth

that has no substitute, clings on, but over time,
has become less a tooth and more a curate's egg,

over which I stand guard. Which reminds me of a cat
I knew who lived behind the great glass architecture

of a doorway relish. I met her through proximity
and habit, hers and ours, which meant we had similar

timetables. I called the cat *Potato* because she was notable
for her coat: a sentimental recipe for a gravy of castaway

bacon with spots of anchor and buried gripe we melted
for cheap cuts of cod, poured as trim for peeled and boiled

reds, the perfect colors of disguise for a cat in a season
of old snow like today, thirty years later, and she still sits

with head tipped to catch the roofline, ready to greet
the sinus of a new winter's day. It meets us now

as the approximate reduction of a devotion,
ignoring even the smell of dinner cans. Even I know

this collapsed stare, authentic to gentleman specialists,
their suede jackets mildewed with rotting field notes,

reminders that anything properly observed can be
mistaken. Because displayed here is an example of a man

who is afraid of rats, and only accurate to seventy percent.

A Theory of Eczema

The doctor said take for example my heart,
where just over the sternum an Eisenhower
of skin emerged overnight. The itching begs

for me, eventually leaves only a rose scar
of Churchill. An episode that lives in a future
where there's no one but the ghost of you.

And on this patch classical time screams by.
Really, it's a killing field, floral with elaborate
errors and less fearsome with maybes.

Each army ignorant of entreaties, of who owns
the land. There the sun isn't a symbol of peace,
and neither force has it decorating their uniforms

or venereal shields. One side wears a tattoo
of ache, the other hosts the itch. I wish I could
tell you that there's a reasonable solution,

but the complete body only provides perspective:
if the spot were a weed, you'd pull up the skin
by the brain. We're all sorry. The uncle

who smells of tar is apologetic. So is my future
self, who also happens to mumble. I wish he'd
turn around, face the prophet, eat his progeny—

and all decreasing fractions of them.

Bobby Fischer Dies during the Whaling Report

The amening heroes

who have tracked the sources of great
rivers leading to death and evil

death, as we would believe, scorned the

mountain streams—
how the flow could resemble stillness

and a ghostly porcelaining (a release

not absolved of farewell or of bidding
farewell). The observer

suddenly the object rushing away

from itself. And sometimes
a reluctant object, a man, say, who forgets

to be human, becomes

a victim of his own private language,
as if someone was translating

but that person is a child standing across

from him on the opposite bank of a raging
arroyo, shouting instruction? It's a case similar

to hearing the cries of a rooster

from another valley. The rooster stands
on the farmer's roof and it is deep night.

The bird is warning the world

that escaped foxes are hunting.
The corrupted declaration wakes you,

without association.

Like a Good Horse

From a distance a gray man waving at no one

seems green as he stands scalloped against, and

sometimes in, the white steam escaping a sulfur

fumarole. Behind them both the fallen curtain

of an alluvial plain. And a dandelion seed,

anchored now to a rusty cat comb, repeats

in the breeze frantic motions of a trapped mayfly.

At this point set aside an understanding of how

a false strawberry vine will go as well

down a wall as across the lawn and ask yourself:

Is the gray man, now on his knees, praying?

And is the seed designed to promote its own

freedom? Be careful in answering. The examples

are neither different nor the same.

Regret, Speckled by Want

I look up at the failing clouds
and dictate yet another epistle to you

but can't remember where one letter
ends and I resume the grim Nirvana.

I live in a cave now that has been lived
in before, its walls carved with glyphs

I do not recognize, the bone tools neatly
arranged as if for me. Beyond a shallow

river, without cobbles, spreads into
a flat stretch of veld only a general

from his saddle could love. Between us:
the general's mount froths at the bit,

chewing out green bubbles that drop,
out of constancy, onto his henchman's

polished boot.

* * *

The dog rose has found itself again,
born of a filament, remembering itself not

from where I pulled it out by the canes,
but from between the gabbro retentions

the length of the declarative alluvium—
where red grasses lean. Within ten years

the roses will subsume the rock, inviting
foxes, and their nervous mating.

* * *

Is it too much of me to ask you to write
me back? Last night I dreamt I was in

a public bath, talking to a dead friend;
I casually turned my head, as one does,

and caught a glimpse of you as you passed
behind me, escorted by the general,

and your only gesture to press a finger
to my spine before you walked away.

Let me be clear: the clouds stream up
from the south in winter, over where he waits.

Should any word arrive from you,
I will walk the black plain,

before picking up the tools
to write my apology.

Vultures and the Constant Application of Them

Their approach lacks sudden-
ness because they waste no light,
because ruination is an activity they
calculate against the terrain,
the brown fescue, thickets of wild honeysuckle,
a sycamore.

The approach is an interaction of opposites,
upon which they wake or sleep. And
it is toward their sleep
you most notice them
gathering in the century oak
they've killed to roost—

the shadow stretching up a patch of lawn
forming an image of their god
they instinctively created.
Even though they have no need for one,
it appears anyway.

Agrimensura of the Mire: Árnessýsla

Uncle, how goes the dacha? I heard the septic
floated up through the ground and that repairs

are stalled because your beloved horses
use it as a scratching post. How is the homeplace

carved out of the moor, through its feathered
lichen, blackberries, and red dagger?

After years of living below the volcano,
I am convinced you own a field of bones.

The house smells of last night's fire when my sister

mistook you for me. What can I say? You were me
in my place. Even after I removed my cap.

And my wife she called your

wife by name. I heard the volcano's ash cloud
blows your way. I can't help but remember

when I visited one summer and there was no hay

to collect, nothing resembling a field even,
and we dug paths to the hen house. The chickens

went mad from the bluster of metallic ticks

across the entire Quonset. The birds moving
around the room like shoals of fish stopped laying.

We wrung each dead and buried them below the manure pile.

Calamity has never been more perfect, you said…You said.
And now you say that the barbed wire sang in the wind,

the notes driven toward the summer house from the ten directions.

You woke to lightning, and the fences stripped of rust.
The foals caught up in them...

And now the ravens call an early parliament and perch

along the fence line, creating a crude map with artifacts
to seek a solution to emptiness: *even when the world is destroyed,*

it is indestructible.

NOTES

"Where I Came Here From" is for my daughter, Eydís.

"The Solitary" is for Isamu Noguchi.

"Antidote to the Chaos of Imagination" is for Norman Dubie.

"An Icelandic Christmas Poem without Animals" is for Beckian Fritz Goldberg.

"Vultures and the Constant Application of Them" is for Hakuun Sokai Geoffrey Barratt.

"Agrimensura of the Mire, Arnessyla" is dedicated to my late uncle Guðmundur Jóhannes Hermanníus, horse breeder, sheep herder, former county sheriff, and agrimensura (surveyor) of Árnes County in southwestern Iceland. I wrote this poem for his 80th birthday in the year of the Eyjafjallajökull eruption.

Christopher Burawa is a poet, translator, high school language arts teacher, and ordained Rinzai Zen Buddhist monk. He received an MFA in poetry from Arizona State University. He has received numerous awards for his work, including an NEA Translation Fellowship, Joy Harjo Poetry Prize, an American-Scandinavian Foundation Creative Writing Research Fellowship, Witter Bynner Poetry Translator Residency, among others. He lives with his wife and daughter in Red Wing, Minnesota.

www.ingramcontent.com/pod-product-compliance
Lightning Source LLC
Chambersburg PA
CBHW022127090426
42743CB00008B/1037